CHICO
and the
VERY BAD and NO GOOD DAY

by Peter Di Lisi
illustrated by Brant David

AuthorHouse™
1663 Liberty Drive
Bloomington, IN 47403
www.authorhouse.com
Phone: 1 (800) 839-8640

Published by AuthorHouse 02/15/2018

ISBN: 978-1-5462-2970-4 (sc)
ISBN: 978-1-5462-2969-8 (e)

Library of Congress Control Number: 2018902101

Print information available on the last page.

authorHOUSE®

CHICO
and the
VERY BAD and NO GOOD DAY

Our story begins with Chico the monkey,

having a very bad and no good day.

It all started when he got up in the morning,

as he went outside to play.

The weather was just terrible outside, and it was really pouring down rain.
Chico couldn't do the things he wanted to, so he just sat down to complain.

After a while Chico started to feeling hungry,
so he went to go find a tasty banana to eat.
Chico loved eating bananas everyday,
to him it was the best kind of treat.

But as Chico looked around he noticed,
there was not one banana in sight.
It seemed that all the other monkeys got there first,
and they ate ever last bite.

Chico started to get very angry,
he lost his temper and appetite.
He stomped his feet in anger,
and gave some of the little birds a bit of a fright.

Chico just wanted to be alone,
so he went to go climb his favourite tree.
But because it was raining so hard it was very wet,
which caused Chico's hands to slip free!

Chico fell all the way to the bottom,
things were not working out for him at all that day.
As he started to get really upset from what happened, he heard a little frog say.

"Why are you feeling so down? Things cannot be all that bad."
Chico turned around and said to him sadly,
"you wouldn't say that if you had the day that I have had."

The little frog looked at Chico and said,

"tell me all about it my friend. "

Chico explained how his day was going,

from the terrible rainy beginning

all the way to the falling end.

The little frog looked at Chico and said,

"well your day is about to change.

You see I happen to have magical powers."

Chico thought this frog was pretty strange.

But as Chico started to float in the air,
he knew there was truth in what
that little frog had said.
Then as he was surrounded by
magical mist, somehow Chico ended up
back in his own bed.

The day seemed to have started
all over, Chico didn't have to
feel sad anymore.
Until Chico realized just one thing...

....It was turning out just like the day before.

Rain pouring down on his head, and there were no bananas to eat.
Not being able to climb his favourite tree, because of his wet hands and feet.

The little frog must have messed up Chico thought, nothing changed at all.
It was just as bad as last time, from when he woke up to when he would fall.

There is just no way to change things," Chico said. "And this is just how my day will be."
The frog looked up at Chico and said, "Not if you change your opinion on what you see."

"I will preform my magic once again," the frog said.
"But this time try to enjoy everything.
The bad things as well as the good ones,
you will see what happiness it brings."

The magic mist started Chico's day once again,
with rain pouring down on top of his head.
But this time Chico decided not to complain,
and go out and play in the rain instead.

Chico had a great time playing in the rain;
jumping and splashing in puddles with his feet.
He really worked up a great appetite,
so he thought he would go find something to eat.

But as he looked around he didn't see any bananas.
He was having so much fun he almost forgot.
That he was sad that all the bananas were already eaten,
but then he saw some berries so he thought he would give them a shot.

Chico has never had these berries before,
he has always picked bananas to eat.
But he tried something new that day and realized,
those new berries tasted pretty sweet.

Chico spent that rainy day smiling,
as he arrived at his favorite tree with a big grin.
The little frog looked up at Chico and ask him,
"So Chico, how has your day been?"

Chico looked at the little frog and said,
"it's been such an awesome day!"
Chico explained that all the bad things still happened,
but told him how he enjoyed his day anyway.

Chico realized that bad things will still happen,
just not to let it get in his way.
If he looked at it a bit differently,
he knew he could still make it an awesome day.

"Sometimes bad things happen,
things that are totally out of our control.
It's important to make the best out of it,
because happiness is our number one goal."

by Peter Di Lisi
illustrated by Brant David

About the Author

Ever since Peter Di Lisi was young, he loved using his imagination in just about everything he did. He is now putting his imagination into a series of children's books that have lovable characters along with some great morals, and told in a fun upbeat rhyming style.

Peter grew up in the small town of Port Perry and has since traveled near and far incorporating things he has learned in life to inspire all his books. The Chico series started when he was working in an elementary school, and the kids fell in love with a puppet monkey named Chico that Peter had in his magic act that he did for the school. After the first story was written Peter quickly started thinking of other adventurers that Chico the monkey would have and that the children could learn from.

Look for these titles and more
peterdilisi.com

CPSIA information can be obtained
at www.ICGtesting.com
Printed in the USA
LVHW07s2240220818
587687LV00004B/5/P